PIANO/VOCAL/CHORDS

MOVIES

TEN YEARS OF MOVIE MUSIC HISTORY

1990-2000

REMEMBERING THE '90s

Project Manager: Carol Cuellar
Art Design: Jorge Paredes
Text By: Fucini Productions, Inc.

CONTENTS

CONTENTS

FORREST GUMP
"Against the Wind"

"My mama always said that life is like a box of chocolates: You never know what you're going to get." With these simple words, Forrest Gump not only dispenses some of the best advice to come out of Hollywood in the '90s, but he also describes the almost mystical sense of mastering fate that's at the heart of this Academy Award-winning film.

From his childhood in the South in the late '50s and early '60s to his almost accidental success as an entrepreneur during the yuppie era, the simple-minded Forrest is swept up by the great events of our time.

True to his mama's words, the box of chocolates that was Forrest's life was full of surprises. Fate has Forrest cross paths with the likes of Elvis, John Lennon, and John Kennedy. However, he is more than a mere victim of fate. A big and impersonal society may move him from the civil rights struggle in the South to the war in Vietnam, but Forrest is no passive observer in his own life.

Although not very bright in the school sense of the word, Forrest knows who he is, and he's at peace with himself. This rock-solid sense of self has given him a fierce determination to grow, regardless of what obstacles must be overcome. Throughout the film, he continues to struggle, the perpetual underdog, beating the odds through sheer force of will.

Of all the great rock and soul songs in the Forrest Gump soundtrack, there is none that better captures the spirit of Forrest himself than the Bob Seger classic "Against the Wind." Like Forrest, this song is about being in control of your own destiny and never giving up, even when the odds seem stacked against you.

The wise, raspy voice of Bob Seger, backed by a haunting piano, seems to capture the quiet dignity of Forrest as portrayed by Tom Hanks. Like Forrest, Seger has traveled great distances over long periods of time when he sings the evocative line, "Seems like yesterday, but it was long ago."

Listening to the gently rolling melody of "Against the Wind," we realize that the artist singing this song agrees with Forrest's mama that life is indeed like a box of chocolates. Regardless of which piece of chocolate comes next, Seger's performance tells us that he will enjoy it to the fullest and "keep riding against the wind."

THE THREE MUSKETEERS
"All for Love"

In the sixteenth-century novel by Alexandre Dumas, the Three Musketeers were Athos, Porthos, and Aramis. For music lovers of the '90s, the swashbuckling trio went by the names Bryan, Rod, and Sting. Rock legends Bryan Adams, Rod Stewart, and Sting performed "All for Love," the feature song in the soundtrack for the 1993 hit film *The Three Musketeers*.

Written by Adams, "All for Love" soared to the top of the U.S. charts and reached the No. 2 position in the UK. No wonder—anyone who has ever been in love can embrace this moving song, which showcases Adams' great talent as a romantic lyricist. From the earliest stage of his career, the Canadian superstar has been able to write and perform songs that convey heartfelt expressions of love without being mushy or overly sentimental.

When Adams is joined in "All for Love" by his two fellow rock icons, the result is a captivating blend of tender devotion and raw emotional power. Like many of the great hits we've enjoyed from Adams, Stewart, and Sting, "All for Love" tugs gently at our emotions with its sweet vulnerability while making our hearts beat more quickly with its undercurrent of passion.

With its touching mix of emotions, "All for Love" is the perfect song for *The Three Musketeers* soundtrack. The same feelings that are captured so well in Adams' words and music are also very evident in the lives of the film's heroes. Played with great verve by Kiefer Sutherland, Charlie Sheen, Oliver Platt, and Chris O'Donnell, the Three Musketeers and their young friend D'Artagnan are loving, caring, devoted, and loyal just like the characters in the song.

The Musketeers are moved by great passions in this film, directed by Stephen Herek. Sure of their emotions and unflinching in their devotion to their cause and one another, they are at times also touchingly vulnerable. After all, the world of the Three Musketeers is an uncertain and sometimes treacherous place. The scheming Cardinal Richelieu has disbanded the Musketeers' order, which was responsible for protecting France's young king. Richelieu is plotting to overthrow the young monarch and claim the throne for himself.

True to the spirit of the swashbuckling hero, the Three Musketeers and D'Artagnan rise to meet the challenge posed by Richelieu. Swords slash and disasters are narrowly averted, but in the end the Musketeers and their cause triumph. The heroes in this film seem to live by a philosophy expressed so well in Adams' lyrics, "When it's love you give . . . then in love you live."

That's a good sentiment for a Musketeer and the rest of us.

ANASTASIA
"At the Beginning"

It is the stuff of legends—a beautiful young princess separated from her doomed royal family in the chaos of a revolution that ends their centuries-old rule of a vast and rich empire. Somewhere in the great expanse of that empire the young princess has disappeared. The months turn into years with no sign of the princess. Is she alive? Has she assumed a new identity, perhaps among the common people? Will she ever reappear to claim her legacy?

Tragedy. Intrigue. Treachery. Doubt. No wonder the story of Anastasia has been told and retold so many times since the fall of the imperial Romanov family in 1917. The haunting legend of the little Russian princess was given a dazzling new twist in 1996 with the release of the animated musical *Anastasia*.

Directed by Don Bluth, the film takes us on a spectacular adventure through the turmoil of the Russian Revolution and the years that follow, as the heroic Anastasia struggles against the evil Rasputin to reclaim her lost past. Children of all ages are captivated by the film's lush animation and the inspired twists and turns of its plot.

Anastasia's epic adventure is given an added emotional dimension by the film's richly powerful and diverse soundtrack. Like the legend behind the film itself, these songs take us through a spectrum of moods, from the grandeur of "Paris Holds the Key" to the gentle yearning of "Once Upon a December."

The vivid tapestry of emotions that is woven through the entire *Anastasia* soundtrack seems to reach its full splendor in the beautifully moving song "At the Beginning." Written by the Tony Award-winning team of Lynn Ahrens and Stephen Flaherty, this song captures many of the qualities that make Anastasia herself so unforgettable. Like the lost princess, "At the Beginning" reminds us that the human spirit, with its ability to hope and love, is a powerful force capable of overcoming any obstacle.

Richard Marx, who arranged "At the Beginning," teams up with Donna Lewis to perform the song, which has quickly become one of our most beloved pop tunes. The voices of these two gifted artists soar together with choir-like force as they celebrate the heroic journey of Anastasia. Like the story of the legendary last princess of a lost empire, the song leaves us endlessly fascinated and longing for more.

THE RUNAWAY BRIDE
"Blue Eyes Blue"

Spencer Tracy and Katherine Hepburn. Richard Burton and Elizabeth Taylor. Every era seems to have at least one film couple that works a special brand of romantic magic on the big screen. In this generation, that title belongs to Richard Gere and Julia Roberts. At the start of the '90s, Gere and Roberts captured our hearts and tickled our collective funny bone in the smash hit *Pretty Woman*. As the decade drew to a close in the summer of 1999, the talented duo charmed us all over again with the release of *Runaway Bride*.

In the movie, Gere plays Ike Graham, a crusty New York newspaper columnist who goes to a small Maryland town to follow up on a story about Maggie Carpenter, played by Roberts, an often-engaged woman with a habit of leaving would-be grooms waiting at the altar. Once Ike arrives in town, the rest of the film is devoted to bringing him and Maggie together.

The ending of this delightful film doesn't take us by surprise, but we certainly have a lot of fun watching Ike and Maggie hook up. This film is meant to be enjoyed in an uncomplicated way, like a picture-perfect summer day in the park with good friends.

A big part of the fun is the soundtrack, which includes songs from a diverse group of artists like the Dixie Chicks, Billy Joel, and Marc Anthony. It was so easy to like the music in this movie that a lot of fans probably decided to buy the soundtrack album before they left the theater.

For many fans, the highlight of this excellent soundtrack was Eric Clapton's "Blue Eyes Blue." A new song written by Diane Warren, "Blue Eyes Blue" showcases Clapton's genius as a guitarist. With its out-of-this-world guitar riffs, this silky smooth folk-pop tune shows us why Clapton is one of the great musicians not only of the '90s but of all time.

The heartfelt lyrics of "Blue Eyes Blue" lend an added dimension to the song. We can enjoy this great musical achievement on many different levels: as the background to an upbeat summer movie, as a catchy and carefree tune in its own right, or as a masterful fusion of different styles by a gifted artist.

Like *Runaway Bride*, which thrives on the interaction between its two charismatic stars, "Blue Eyes Blue" is elevated by the special magic that exists between Eric Clapton and his guitar.

EVITA
"Don't Cry for Me Argentina"

She already established herself as a rock superstar, a video diva, and a cultural phenomenon, but could Madonna carry the lead role in a serious musical? Some critics voiced this concern in November 1996 when *Evita* was released. However, as she did so often during the '90s, Madonna proved that those who pegged her as "only a rock star" had grossly underestimated her spectacular natural talents.

Even Madonna's most skeptical critics were left humbled and awestruck by her powerfully moving performance as the star-crossed Eva Peron in the film version of the musical *Evita*. With her characteristic passion, Madonna immersed herself in the role of Eva, the beautiful Argentinean who rose from poverty to become the wife of dictator Juan Peron.

Madonna didn't just play the lead role in this film, she became Eva, embracing this strong and independent woman's passions and fears and making them her own. Everything about Madonna in this film, from her make-up to the way she moved and held her body to the subtlest nuance of her facial expressions, showed how thoroughly she absorbed the character of Eva Peron.

At no time were Madonna's feelings for and identification with Eva more evident than when she sang "Don't Cry for Me Argentina," the signature song of this memorable musical. Singing from the depths of her own heart and soul, Madonna provided us with an intimate sense of Eva's complex emotions. In a solemn yet seductive voice, she seemed to carry the weight of Eva's long personal journey in her performance.

Listening to Madonna sing gave us a deeply personal sense of the struggles in Eva Peron's life and the price that her rise to fame extracted from her. It was as if Madonna's performance opened a window into the soul of Eva Peron to show us how far this remarkable woman came and the sacrifices she made along the way.

A strong and intelligent woman like Madonna, Eva Peron understood the difficulties she faced in a "man's world." With dignity and grace, Eva stood ready to meet whatever fate had in store for her. She did not need Argentina to cry for her because she relied on her own unshakable belief in herself. Recognizing this part of Eva Peron, Madonna projects a calm, philosophical sense of acceptance in her performance of "Don't Cry for Me Argentina." Ultimately, this song is a fitting tribute to one remarkable woman from another.

THE PREACHER'S WIFE
"I Believe in You and Me"

Handsome Denzel Washington plays an angel in *The Preacher's Wife*, but the halo in this 1996 film is worn by Whitney Houston. Playing Julia Biggs, the wise and understanding wife of preacher Henry Biggs (Courtney B. Vance), Houston shows us why she became one of the most successful film and recording stars of the '90s. During the decade, Houston starred in three films (*The Bodyguard* and *Waiting to Exhale* are the other two). Aside from being runaway box-office smashes, all three films produced wildly successful soundtrack albums and hit singles.

Houston's singing and acting radiate a sense of pure magic throughout *The Preacher's Wife*, a stylish remake of the 1947 Academy Award-winner, *The Bishop's Wife*, which starred Cary Grant. The beautiful superstar is at her spellbinding best in the film when, as Julia Biggs, she sings "I Believe in You and Me" during a visit to Jazzie's nightclub.

Julia (Houston) was taken to the club by Dudley, a sharp-dressed angel played by Washington, who had come to New York from heaven to help the Reverend Biggs save his Baptist church as well as his marriage. When events keep the reverend away from home, Dudley finds himself spending more time alone with Julia.

Things get complicated when Dudley starts falling for Julia. His infatuation is easy to understand. Julia Biggs not only has the face of an angel, but she also has a sweet and caring heart to match. With a graceful ease that only an actress of Houston's ability can convey, Julia balances the quiet dignity of being the preacher's wife with the deep currents of passion that run through her heart.

All of the wonderful qualities that draw Dudley to Julia come to the forefront when she sings "I Believe in You and Me." Houston uses her crystalline voice like a divine instrument as she wraps the enthralled Dudley (as well as the audience) in the deeply romantic mood of the song. Julia's angelic face glows with emotions when she sings, pulling us further into this magical moment.

"I Believe in You and Me," which reached No. 4 on the U.S. charts, is an outstanding song in its own right. Its moving melody and lyrics are a celebration of love's great power: "I believe in miracles. And love is a miracle."

As we listen to Julia sing these lines at Jazzie's, we wonder about the source of her passion. Is it her husband? Dudley? Or simply the miracle we call love? We will never know with certainty—and this uncertainty is one of the things that makes this a special song in a special scene, performed by a great artist.

MY BEST FRIEND'S WEDDING
"I Say a Little Prayer"

The 1997 box-office hit *My Best Friend's Wedding* is all about reclaiming things. Julianne Potter, the film's main character (played beautifully by Julia Roberts), is a hard-driving 28-year-old restaurant writer who moves through life without forming any lasting attachments.

Julianne's world is turned upside down when she receives a call from her former college buddy, the handsome Michael O'Neal (Dermot Mulroney), inviting her to his upcoming wedding to the gorgeous and wealthy Kimmy Wallace (Cameron Diaz). Back in college, Julianne and Michael had promised they would marry each other if neither had found a suitable mate by the time they were 28. Unfortunately, now that they have reached the magic age, Michael plans to marry someone else.

For the remainder of this rollicking romantic comedy, Julianne plots to win back the man whom she regards as rightfully belonging to her. The buoyant soundtrack we hear as we follow Julianne's schemes provides us with a sense of rediscovery as well. However, instead of reclaiming a lost lover, we have the pleasure of renewing our acquaintance with some of the best pop music of an earlier generation.

Featuring many songs written by Burt Bacharach and Hal David, the soundtrack is a joyous, unabashed celebration of the '60s pop scene. Unlike many retro soundtracks, though, this one does much more than revisit familiar old standards. The classic tunes that serve as the musical backdrop for this film have a decidedly '90s twist. Instead of being done by the original artists, many of the songs are performed by superstars of this era. There are Ani DiFranco singing "Wishin' and Hopin'," Mary-Chapin Carpenter covering "I'll Never Fall in Love Again," and many more.

The spirit of the soundtrack and the film itself really come to life in "I Say a Little Prayer." There are actually two different versions of this song on the soundtrack. In one version, the first cut on the soundtrack album, Jamaican-born Diana King serves up an upbeat reggae rendition of the song. As she did in her hit "Stir It Up," King seems to bring her own unique emotional energy to every lick, inviting us to share in the fun she's obviously having with this classic hit.

Also having fun with "I Say a Little Prayer" is the cast of *My Best Friend's Wedding*. Julia Roberts, Cameron Diaz, and Dermot Mulroney join in a free-wheeling, upbeat rendition of the song. As singers, these film stars can't match the vocals of Diana King, but their energy and enthusiasm are contagious, and they sound great. After all, "I Say a Little Prayer" is the kind of expansive, generous song that invites everyone to sing along. That's as true today as it was in the '60s.

SCHINDLER'S LIST
"Theme From Schindler's List"

At the start of the '90s, John Williams was already one of the most successful composers of film scores in history. A familiar sight to viewers of the Oscars on television, Williams won Best Film Score Academy Awards for *Fiddler on the Roof, Jaws, Close Encounters, Star Wars, E.T.,* and other films. His rousing, full-bodied romantic overtures were instantly recognizable to fans of adventure films like *Indiana Jones.*

In 1993, Williams departed from his tried-and-true "big flourish" formula when he composed the score for Steven Spielberg's important and deeply moving Holocaust drama *Schindler's List.* A dark, haunting, and gripping film, *Schindler's List* addresses the unspeakable horror of the Holocaust by telling the story of a Nazi industrialist who maneuvers to save more than 1,000 Jewish workers from certain death in work camps as World War II draws to a close.

No one who saw this film is likely to forget Spielberg's unsettling images. Nor are they likely to forget the music that provides a restrained yet emotionally charged backdrop to this tragic story. In composing the score for *Schindler's List,* Williams reveals another, more solemn, side of his musical genius. The bravado that his legions of fans have come to expect from his film scores is nowhere to be found. In its place, Williams has given us a profound and reflective work that is both deeply sad and serenely uplifting at the same time.

In "Theme From Schindler's List," Williams establishes the emotional undercurrent of Spielberg's tragic masterpiece. Listening to his evocative melody gives us a chilling sense of foreboding as we watch the film's mournful events unfold. Yet, just as Spielberg does in the film, Williams manages to preserve and honor the dignity of this tragedy's victims through his music. In so doing, his music supports the ray of hope that shines through the dark drama.

Working in harmony with the film, Williams' score captures the surreal sense that surrounds Schindler (played by Liam Neeson) and Jewish prisoner Itzhak Stern (Ben Kingsley) as they go about their work of saving lives in the middle of a real-world nightmare. From a dramatic standpoint, the music also heightens the level of suspense at several points during the film.

Williams' music is made even more compelling by the violin performance of Itzhak Perlman. At times, the masterful Perlman seems to make his violin sigh with a sad, heavy voice weighed down by the suffering of millions of Holocaust victims. Listening to Perlman's performance, we get the impression that the great violinist and the famous composer have read one another's minds. Through their close collaboration, they take us into the heart of darkness while preserving our sense of human dignity. Together with Spielberg, they have created a work of art that honors the victims of the Holocaust and offers us hope that humankind can learn from the past.

From the Original Motion Picture Soundtrack "THE THREE MUSKETEERS"

ALL FOR LOVE

Written by
BRYAN ADAMS, ROBERT JOHN "MUTT" LANGE
and MICHAEL KAMEN

All for Love - 6 - 1

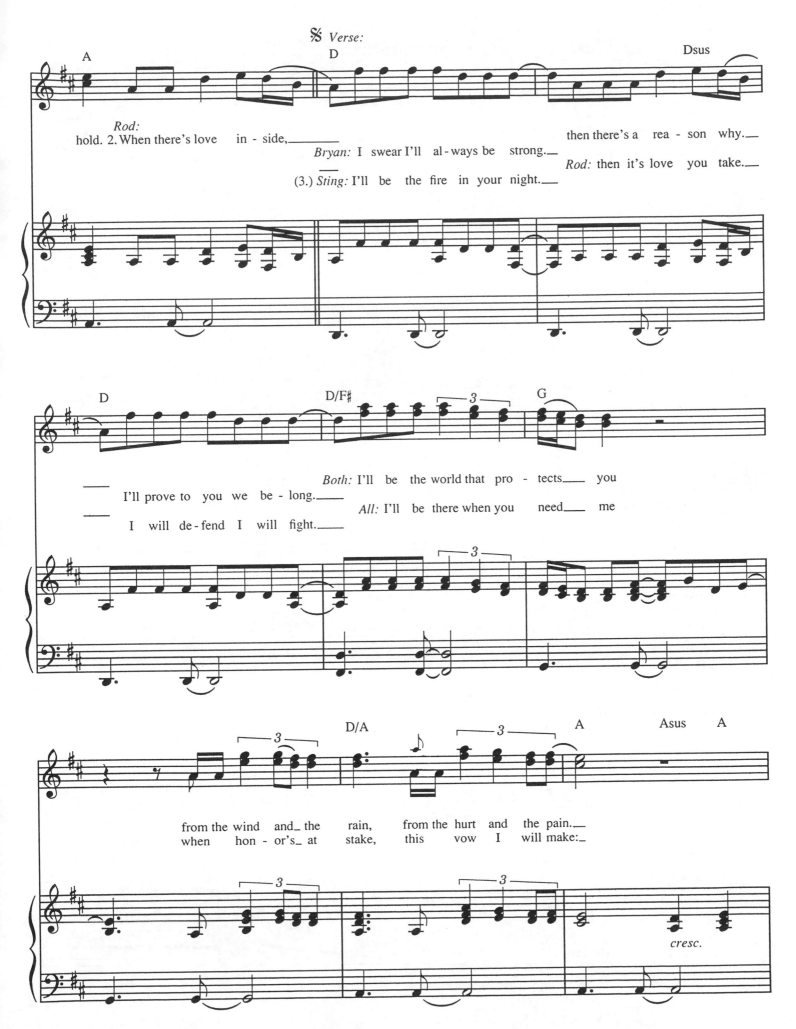

14

16

THE ANIMAL SONG

Words and Music by
DARREN HAYES and DANIEL JONES

The Animal Song - 8 - 1

wind in____ my hair and____ the sand at____ my feet.____

— Ah, ah, ah, how. Ah, ah, ah, how.

Verses 2 & 3:

2. I've been hav - ing dif - fi - cul - ties keep - ing to____ my - self.
   su - per - stars and can - ni - bals____ are run - ning through____ your head.

Feel - ings and e - mo - tions bet - ter left____ up - on____ the shelf.____
Tel - e - vi - sion freak____ show, cops and rob - bers ev - 'ry - where.____

AGAINST THE WIND

Words and Music by
BOB SEGER

Medium Rock beat

It seems like yes - ter - day, ___
And the years rolled slow - ly past. ___

Instrumental ___

but it was long a - go. ___
And I found my - self a - lone, ___

Against the Wind - 5 - 1

From the Fox 2000 Motion Picture "ANYWHERE BUT HERE"

ANYWHERE BUT HERE

Words and Music by
k.d. lang and RICK NOWELS

Anywhere But Here - 5 - 1

Bridge:

Cal - i - for - nia's gon - na be___ the place___

___ for me.___

Do do do do do do do,

From the Twentieth Century-Fox Motion Picture "ANASTASIA"

AT THE BEGINNING

Lyrics by
LYNN AHRENS

Music by
STEPHEN FLAHERTY

1. We were stran-gers start-ing out on a jour-ney, nev-er dream-ing what we'd

have to go through.___ Now here we are and I'm sud-den-ly stand-ing

At the Beginning - 7 - 1

42

on._____ Start-ing out on a jour-ney. Life is a road, and I want to keep go-ing.

Love is a riv-er, I wan-na keep flow-ing. In the end, I wan-na be stand-ing at the be-gin-ning____

____ with____ you._____

From the Motion Picture RUNAWAY BRIDE
BLUE EYES BLUE

Words and Music by
DIANE WARREN

From the Universal Motion Picture "THE BEST MAN"

THE BEST MAN I CAN BE

Slowly ♩ = 72

Words and Music by
JAMES WRIGHT, JAMES HARRIS III and
TERRY LEWIS

Verse:

1. Stand-ing here a - lone,___ try'n' to face an - oth - er day.___
2. *See additional lyrics*

Got - ta stay strong___ to en - dure this pain___ I'm deal-

The Best Man I Can Be - 6 - 1

The Best Man I Can Be - 6 - 4

Repeat as desired (vocal ad lib.) | Last time

(Be the best man.)

Verse 2:
I made a big mistake
And I'm feeling so ashamed.
And I don't wanna lose my friendship over it.
I've got to keep the faith.
'Cause I'm still your boy, I've got you back.
That ain't never, never, never gonna change.
So I just can't hide the truth
And keep smiling in your face.
(To Chorus:)

CAN'T TAKE MY EYES OFF OF YOU

Words and Music by
BOB CREWE and BOB GAUDIO

Moderate tempo

Can't Take My Eyes off of You - 3 - 1

CONTACT
(Main Title)

Written and Composed by
ALAN SILVESTRI

Moderately slow ♩ = 88

(with pedal)

Contact - 3 - 1

COUNT ON ME

Words and Music by
BABYFACE, WHITNEY HOUSTON
and MICHAEL HOUSTON

Count on me _ through thick _ and thin, a friend- -ship that _ will nev- er end. When you _ are weak, _ I will _ be strong, _ help- ing you _ to car- ry on. _ Call on me, _ I will _ be there. _

Count on Me - 6 - 1

DOE EYES
(Love Theme from "The Bridges of Madison County")

Composed by
LENNIE NIEHAUS and
CLINT EASTWOOD

Doe Eyes - 4 - 1

DON'T CRY FOR ME ARGENTINA

Words by
TIM RICE

Music by
ANDREW LLOYD WEBBER

And as for for-tune and as for fame, I nev-er in-vit-ed them in, though it seemed to the world they were all I de-sired. They are il-lu-sions, ___ they're not the so-lu-tions they prom-ised to be. The

Don't Cry for Me Argentina - 8 - 8

Music From and Inspired By the Motion Picture POKÉMON - THE FIRST MOVIE

DON'T SAY YOU LOVE ME

Words and Music by
MARION RAVN, MARIT LARSEN,
PETER ZIZZO and JIMMY BRALOWER

Chorus:

Don't say you love me; you don't e - ven know me. If you real - ly want me, then give me some time. Don't go there, ba - by, not be - fore I'm read - y.

Don't say your heart's in a hur - ry. It's not like we're gon - na get mar - ried.

Don't say you love me; you___ don't e - ven know me, ba - by._____ Ba - by,

don't say___ you love me,___ hey,_____ ba - by.___
(Don't say you love me; you___ don't e - ven know me. If___ you real - ly want me, then

Give me some___ time.___
give me some time.___

Chorus:

Don't say you love me; you___ don't e - ven know me. If___
time.

___ you real - ly want me, then give me some time.___

Don't go there, ba - by, not___ be - fore I'm read - y. Don't say your heart's__ in a hur - ry.

Repeat ad lib. and fade

It's not like we're gon - na get mar - ried. Give me, give me some__

From the New Line Cinema Motion Picture "SET IT OFF"

DON'T LET GO (LOVE)

Words and Music by
ANDREA MARTIN, IVAN MATIAS,
MARQUEZE ETHERIDGE and ORGANIZED NOIZE

Verse:

1. I of-ten tell my-self that we could be more than just friends. I know you think that if we
2. I of-ten fan-ta-size the stars a-bove are watch-ing. They know my heart, how I speak to

move too soon, it would all end._ I live in mis-er-y_ when you're not a-round._
you is like on-ly lov-ers do. If I could wear your clothes, I'd pre-tend I was you,_

And I won't be sat-is-fied_ till we're tak-ing those vows._ } There'll be some
and lose con-trol._ Oh.

Bridge:

love mak-ing, heart-break-ing, soul shak-ing love._

FAITH OF THE HEART

Words and Music by
DIANE WARREN

94

From the Motion Picture "MICHAEL"

FEELS LIKE HOME

Words and Music by
RANDY NEWMAN

Verse 2:
A window breaks down a long, dark street,
And a siren wails in the night.
But I'm alright 'cause I have you here with me,
And I can almost see through the dark, there's a light.
If you knew how much this moment means to me,
And how long I've waited for your touch.
If you knew how happy you are making me,
I've never thought I'd love anyone so much.
(To Chorus:)

From the Motion Picture "G.I. JANE"

GOODBYE

Words and Music by
STEVE EARLE

Goodbye - 5 - 1

I re - call___ au - tumn nights down___ in

Mex - i - co,___ one place I___ might nev - er go___

in my life___ a - gain.

GOTHAM CITY

Words and Music by
R. KELLY

1. Look-ing o-ver the sky-line of____ the cit-y.____
2. Sleep-ing a-wake be-cause____ of fear.____

Gotham City - 5 - 1

From the Motion Picture "MICHAEL"

HEAVEN IS MY HOME

Words and Music by
RANDY NEWMAN

Chorus:

From the Motion Picture "SILENT FALL"

HEALING

Words and Music by
GLEN ALLEN, KILTE REEVES
and ED BERGHOFF

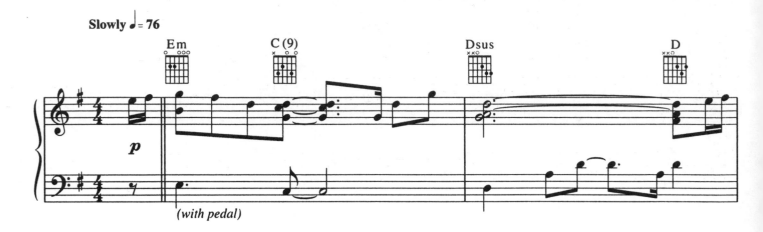

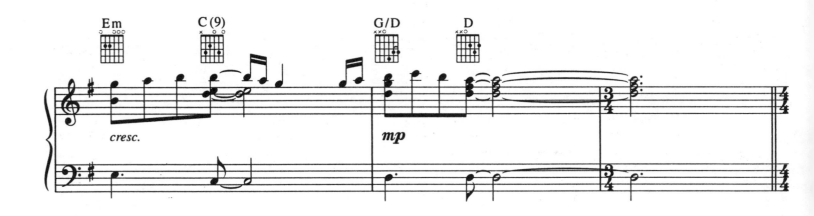

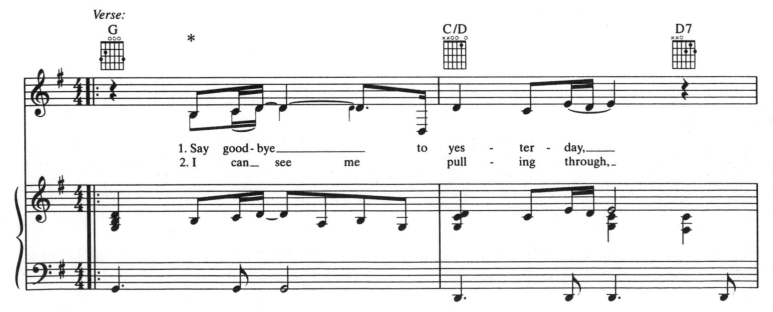

1. Say good-bye_____ to yes - ter - day,_____
2. I can_ see me pull - ing through,_

*2nd verse sung 8va

Healing - 6 - 1

heal - ing.____

heal - ing,____ yeah.____

Bridge:

The chap-ter's been writ - ten,____ it's

Theme from Columbia Pictures Feature Film "HERO"

HEART OF A HERO

Words and Music by
LUTHER VANDROSS

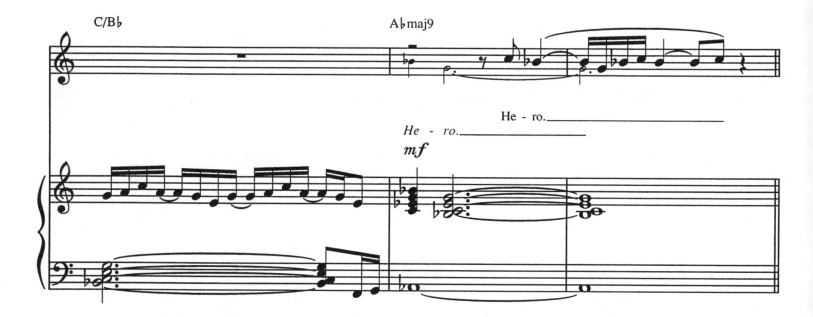

He - ro._____

He - ro._____

Verse:

1. Some-one___ a - bove_____ keeps send - ing___ us love.___
2. If you're a friend_____ to ev - er - y man,___

Heart of a Hero - 6 - 1

Chorus:

"Oh, hap - py day!__ Life is__ for us,__ but life with - out love_ is__ a ze-
"Oh, hap - py day!__ This world is__ for us,__ but a world with - out love_ is__ a ze-

- ro."_____ Sing_ it to-geth - er, "Oh, hap - py day!"_ I heard some-one say,_ "In -
- ro."__ There ain't_ noth-ing to it. "Oh, hap - py day!_ Give love to__ some-one_ and

side ev - 'ry heart_ is_ a he - ro._____ You're_ a he - ro."_____
you'll have_ the heart_ of__ a he - ro._____ You're_ a he - ro."_____

From the Fox 2000 Motion Picture ANNA AND THE KING

HOW CAN I NOT LOVE YOU

Music and Lyric by
GEORGE FENTON,
KENNETH "BABYFACE" EDMONDS
and ROBERT KRAFT

Chorus:

From the Original Soundtrack Album "THE PREACHER'S WIFE"

I BELIEVE IN YOU AND ME

Words and Music by
SANDY LINZER and DAVID WOLFERT

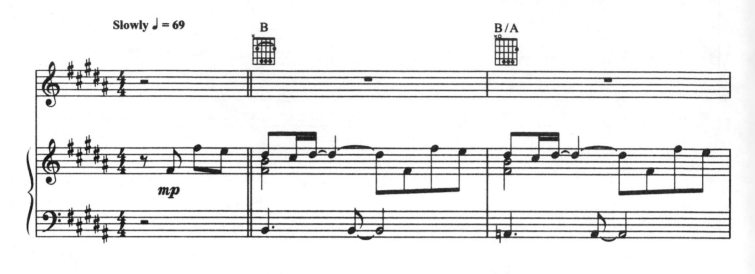

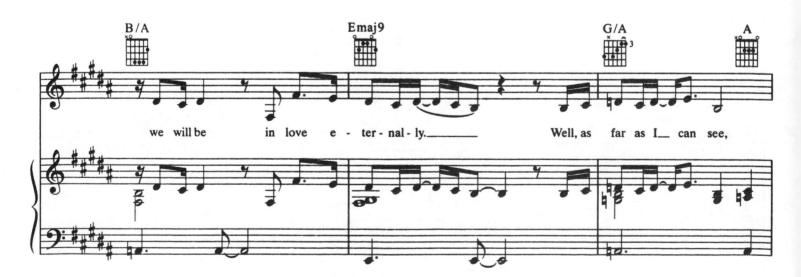

I Believe in You and Me - 4 - 1

Verse 2:

I will never leave your side,

I will never hurt your pride.

When all the chips are down,

I will always be around,

Just to be right where you are, my love.

Oh, I love you, boy.

I will never leave you out,

I will always let you in

To places no one has ever been.

Deep inside, can't you see?

I believe in you and me.

(To Bridge:)

I CROSS MY HEART

Words and Music by
STEVE DORFF and ERIC KAZ

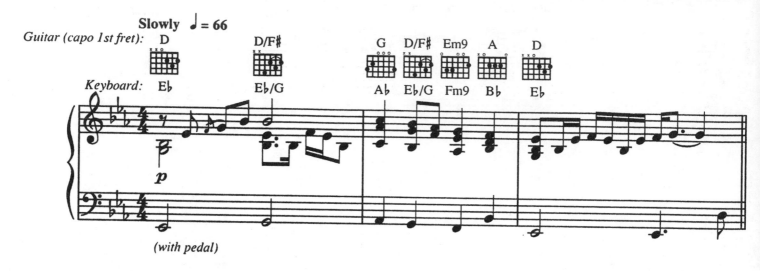

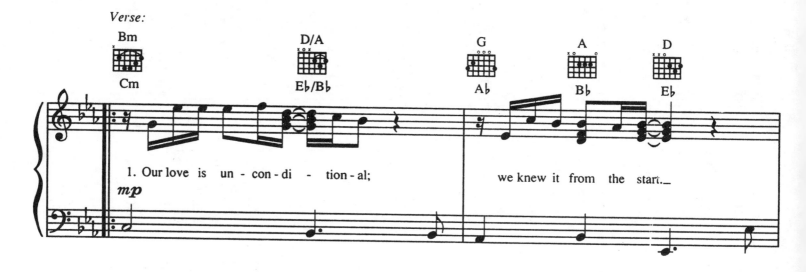

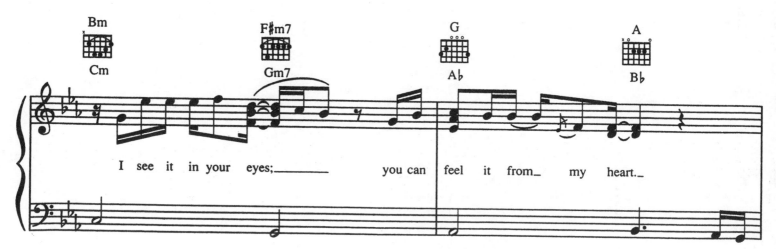

I Cross My Heart - 4 - 1

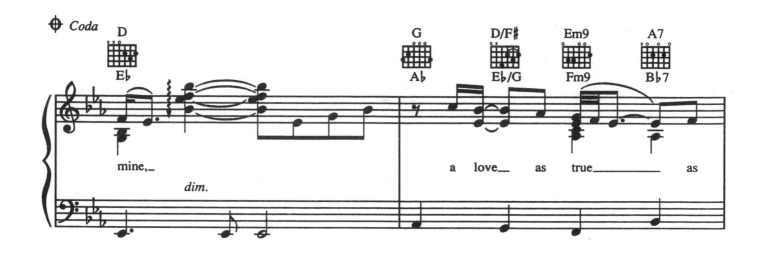

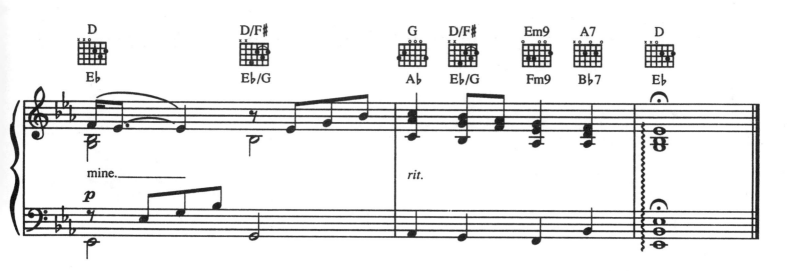

Verse 2:
You will always be the miracle
That makes my life complete;
And as long as there's a breath in me,
I'll make yours just as sweet.
As we look into the future,
It's as far as we can see,
So let's make each tomorrow
Be the best that it can be.
(To Chorus:)

I BELIEVE I CAN FLY

Words and Music by
R. KELLY

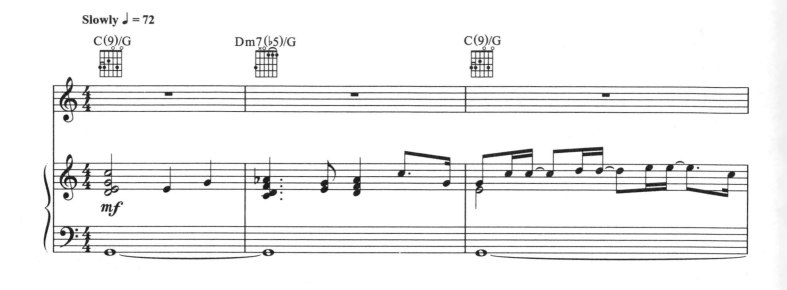

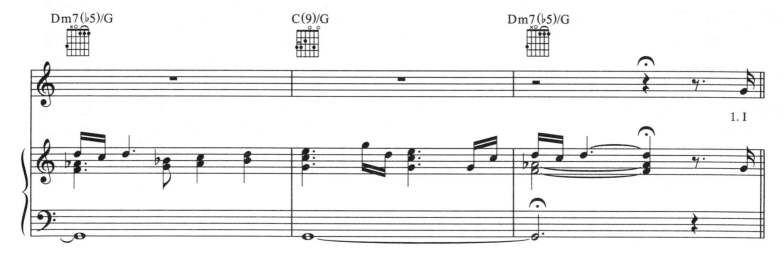

Verse:

used to think that I could not go on, and life was noth-ing but an aw- ful

I was on the verge of break-ing down. Some- times si - lence can seem so

I Believe I Can Fly - 5 - 1

I TURN TO YOU

Words and Music by
DIANE WARREN

Slowly ♩ = 72

From "MY BEST FRIEND'S WEDDING"

I SAY A LITTLE PRAYER

Words by
HAL DAVID

Music by
BURT BACHARACH

I Say a Little Prayer - 6 - 2

Chorus:

ev - er, for - ev - er, you'll stay in my heart___ and I will love you. For -

ev - er and ev - er, we nev - er will part,___ oh, how I'll love you. To -

geth - er, to - geth - er, that's how it should be.___ To live with - out you would

1.

on - ly mean heart - break for me.

IF GOD WILL SEND HIS ANGELS

Music by
U2

Lyrics by
BONO and THE EDGE

If God Will Send His Angels - 8 - 1

To Coda ⊕

where is___ the hope   and where is___ the faith   and the love?

What's that you say to me? What's love?   Light up your Christ-mas tree, the

next   min-ute you're blow-in'___ a fuse.___   A car-toon net-work turns

Repeat ad lib. and fade

I'M STILL IN LOVE WITH YOU

Words and Music by
AL GREEN, WILLIE MITCHELL
and AL JACKSON, JR.

I'm Still in Love With You - 4 - 1

Verse 3:
When I look in your eyes throughout all these years,
How I see me loving you and you loving me.
And it seems to me that I'm wrapped up in your love.
Baby, don't you know that I'm still in love, shonuff in love with you.

Music from THE PRINCE OF EGYPT - INSPIRATIONAL

I WILL GET THERE

Words and Music by
DIANE WARREN

*Recorded a half step lower.

I Will Get There - 7 - 1

Bridge:

Get there.__ Get there.
Well, the night is cold__ and__ dark,_____ but some-

where the sun__ is shin - ing. And I'll feel it shine__ on__ me.__

I'll keep try - ing._____ I'll keep

try - ing._____

cresc.

Chorus:

From the Twentieth Century Fox Motion Picture "THE EDGE"

LOST IN THE WILD

Composed by
JERRY GOLDSMITH

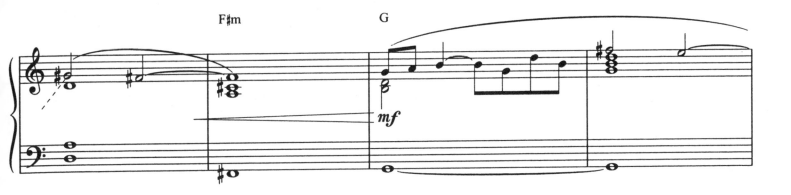

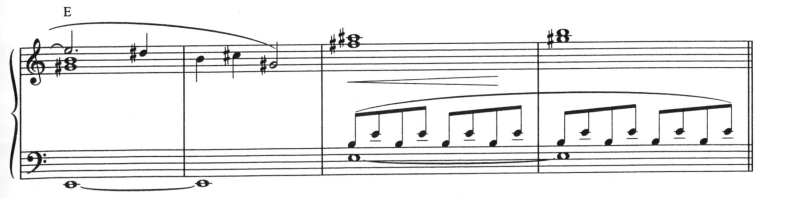

Lost in the Wild - 3 - 1

JOURNEY TO THE PAST

Lyrics by
LYNN AHRENS

Music by
STEPHEN FLAHERTY

1. Heart, don't__ fail__ me now. Cour - age,__ don't__
2. Some - where__ down__ this road, I know__ some -

Journey to the Past - 8 - 1

184

186

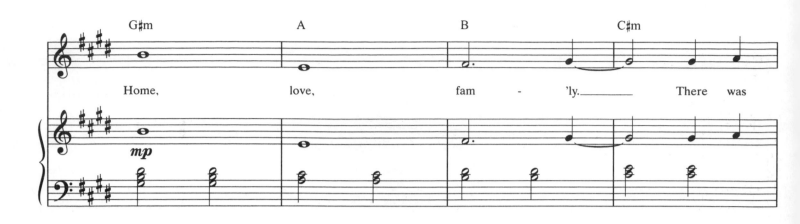

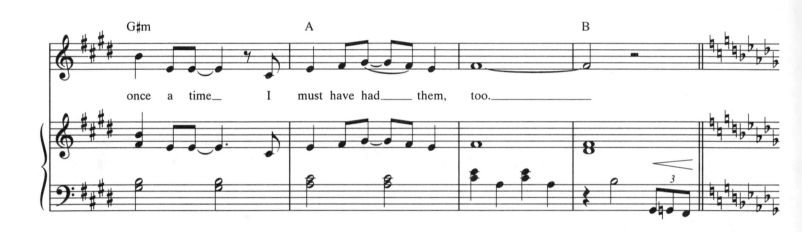

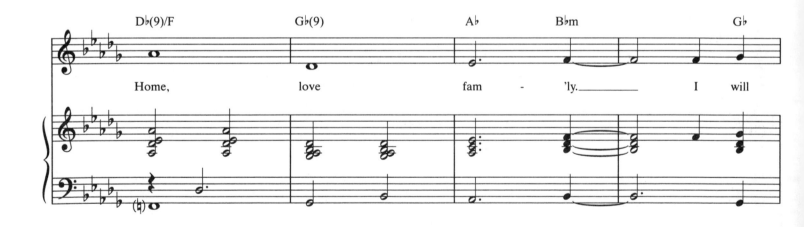

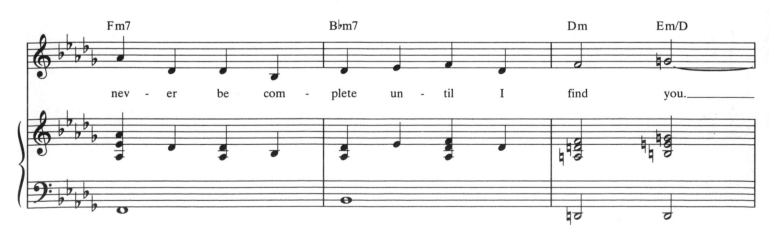

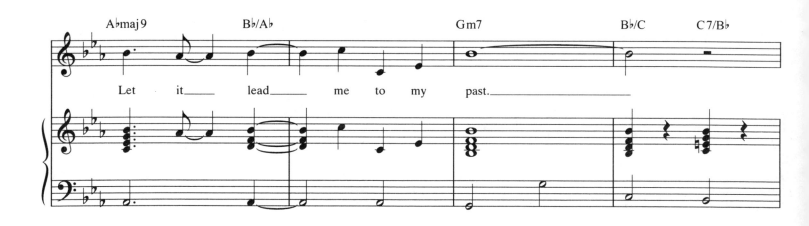

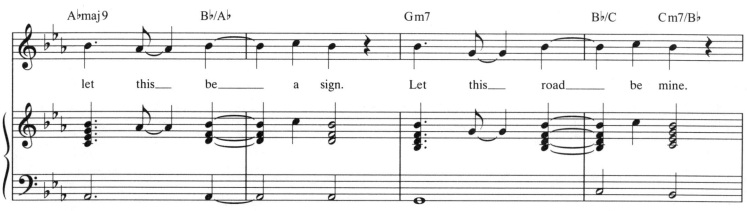

JUST CAUSE
(MAIN TITLE)

Composed by
JAMES NEWTON HOWARD

From the Original Motion Picture Soundtrack "8 SECONDS"

LANE'S THEME

Composed by
BILL CONTI

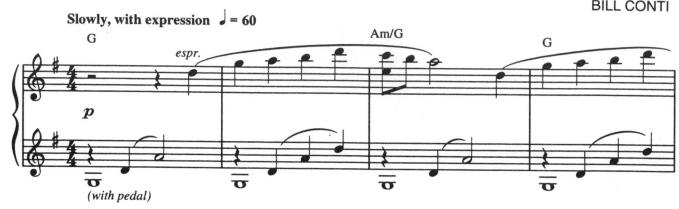

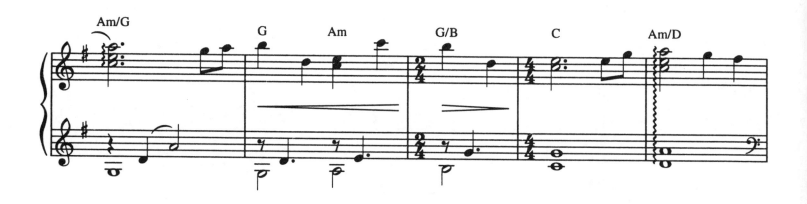

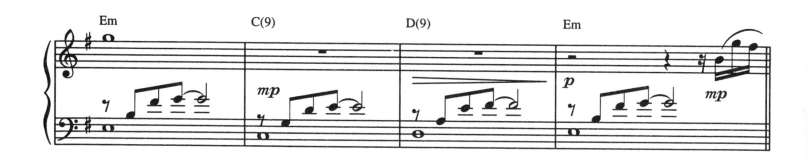

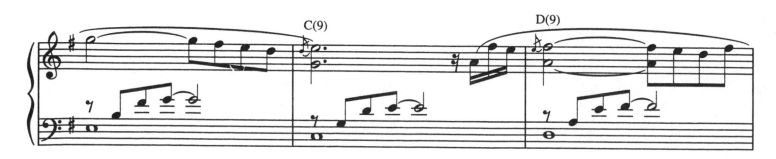

Lane's Theme - 4 - 1

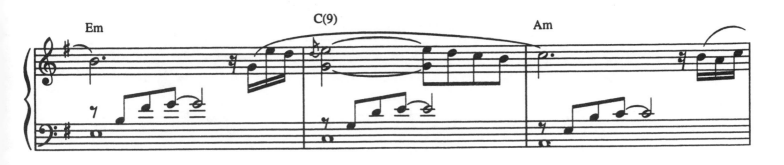

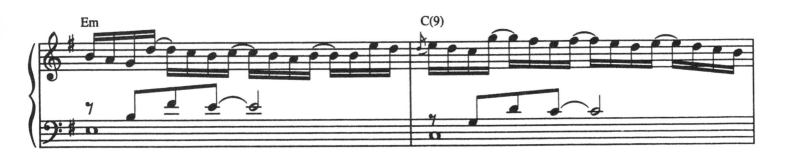

Lane's Theme - 4 - 2

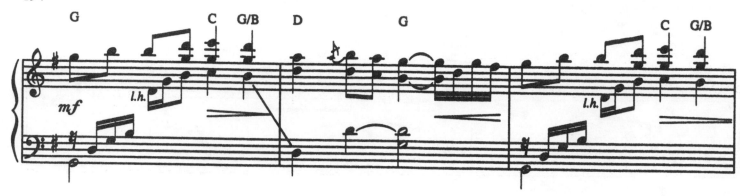

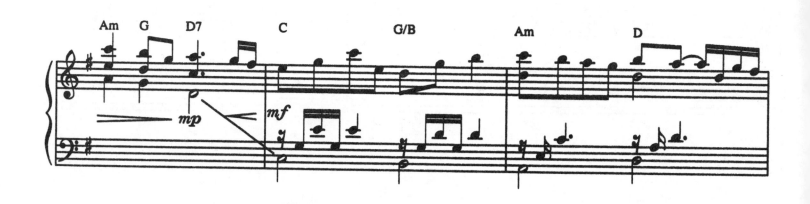

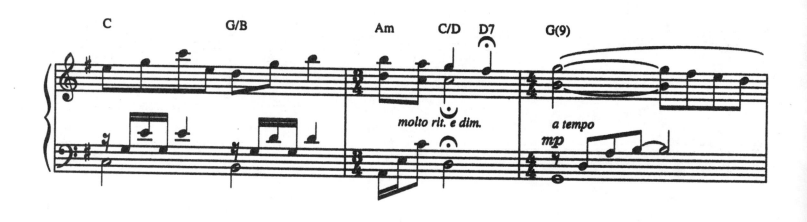

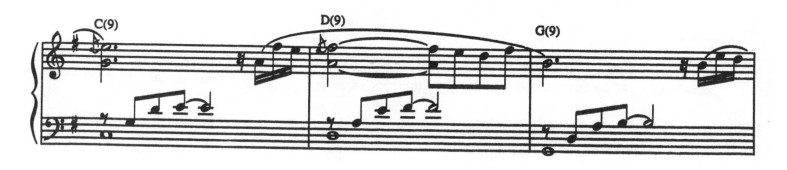

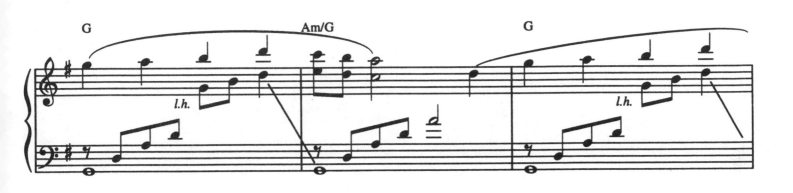

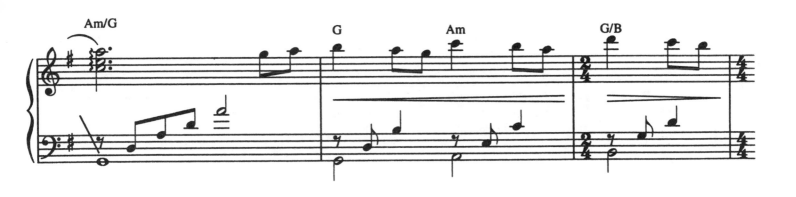

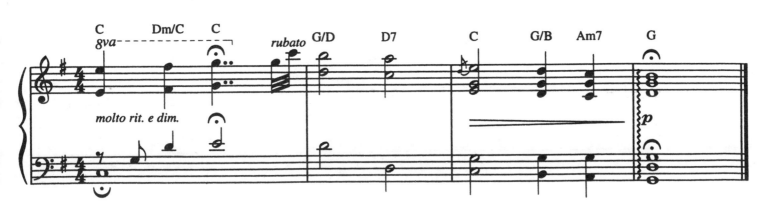

Lane's Theme - 4 - 4

LIFE IN MONO

Words by
MARTIN VIRGO

Music by
MARTIN VIRGO and JOHN BARRY

Verse:

1. The stran - ger___ sang a theme   from some-one else's_
2. The tree - lined_ av - e - nue   be - gins to fade from

dream.   The leaves be - gan to   fall
view.   Drown - ing past re - grets

Life in Mono - 4 - 1

LOVING YOU IS ALL I KNOW

Words and Music by
DIANE WARREN

Loving You Is All I Know - 4 - 1

Verse 4:

And know-ing that, I guess___ I know e - nough.

nough. 4. I don't un-der-stand___ how the sun keeps shin - ing.___ And I don't___

___ un-der - stand___ why the sea-sons change.___ And I don't___ have a clue___

what makes the riv - ers flow. Lov-ing you is all I___ know.

Verse 2:
I can't tell you why stars come out in the evening,
And I can't tell you where they go when they're gone.
And I don't have a clue what makes a flower grow.
Loving you is all I know.
(To Chorus:)

Verse 3:
I can't really say if there is a heaven,
But I feel like it's here when I feel you near me, baby.
I'm not sure of that much, but that's just how it goes.
Loving you is all I know.
(To Chorus:)

From the Miramax Motion Picture "Music Of The Heart"

MUSIC OF MY HEART

Words and Music by
DIANE WARREN

hope for some-thing bet - ter and made me reach for some-thing more.__
one who knew__ me bet - ter than an - y - one ev - er will__ a - gain.__ }You taught me to run,__

Chorus:

__ you taught me to fly,__ helped me to free__ the me__ in - side.__ Helped me hear the

mu - sic of__ my heart. Helped me hear the mu - sic of__ my heart. You o-pened my

eyes, you o-pened the door__ to some-thing I've nev - er known__ be - fore. And your

NOW AND FOREVER

Music and Lyrics by
RICHARD MARX

1. When - ev - er I'm wear - y___ from the bat - tles that rage in my
2. Some-times I'm just hold you,___ too caught up in me to

head, you make sense of mad - ness when my
see I'm hold - ing a for - tune that

san - i - ty hangs by a thread. I lose my way,___
heav-en has giv - en to me. I'll try to show___

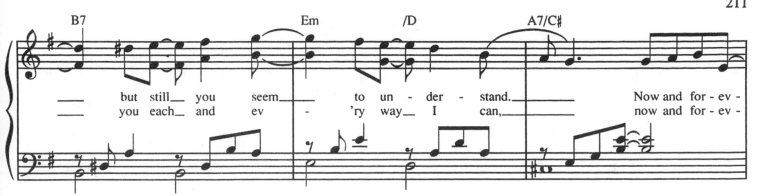

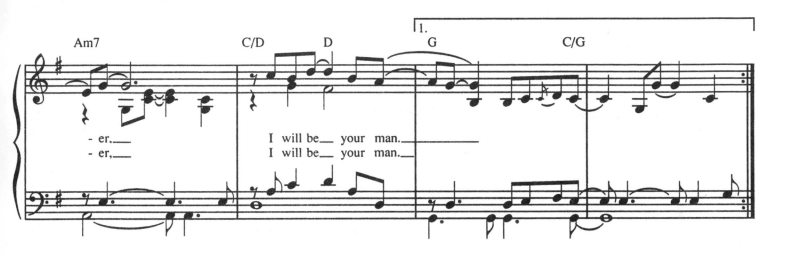

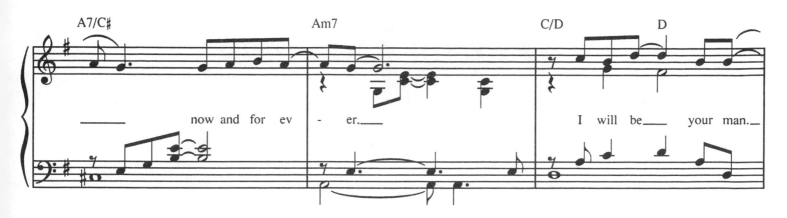

now and for ev - er.___ I will be___ your man.___

Now and for - ev - er,

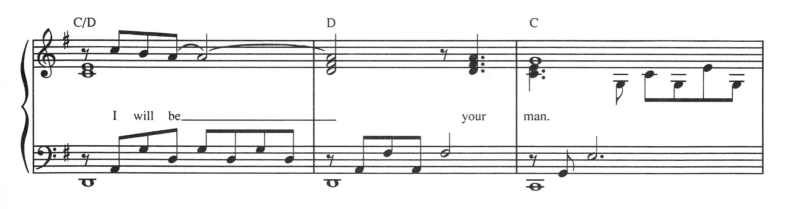

I will be_____ your man.

poco rit. e dim.

mp

From the Motion Picture "THE PAPER"

MAKE UP YOUR MIND

Written by RANDY NEWMAN

I know why peo-ple all o - ver are dis-ap-point-ed with me.__

Eb7

D7 Db7 C7 Db7 D7

When I get up I want down,__

Eb7

D7 Db7 C7 Db6 Eb7

when I got thin I want fat, fat, fat, fat. When I__ get square I want

D7 Db7 C7 Db7 D7 C7/E

F7(#5)

round, when I got this I want that. You bet - ter make up your mind.__

makes me feel so God damn sad I want to cry.

This lit-tle pig-gy went to the mar-ket,

that lit - tle pig - gy got caught up and put in the zoo.___

Last lit - tle pig - gy went "Wa, wa, wa, wa, wa, wa,"

'cause he did - n't know what he was s'posed to do.___

Gm   Dm/F   Eb6   Bb/D   Eb6

Comes a time in ev - 'ry man's life when he must de - cide

ONCE UPON A DECEMBER

Lyrics by
LYNN AHRENS

Music by
STEPHEN FLAHERTY

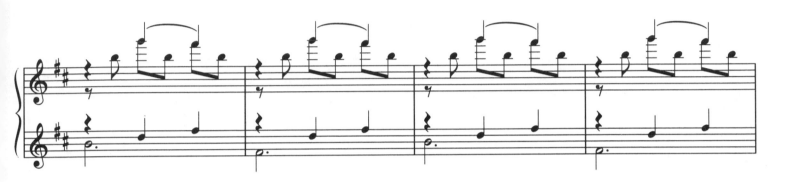

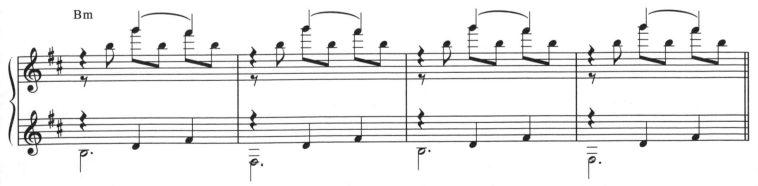

Once Upon a December - 7 - 1

226

THE PRAYER

Italian Lyric by
ALBERTO TESTA and TONY RENIS

Words and Music by
CAROLE BAYER SAGER and DAVID FOSTER

Verse 3:

From the Universal Motion Picture "CASPER"

REMEMBER ME THIS WAY

Lyrics by
LINDA THOMPSON

Music by
DAVID FOSTER

Remember Me This Way - 6 - 1

Verse 2:

2. I don't need eyes_ to see the love_ you bring to

me no mat - ter where_ I go.

Coda

way.____ Re - mem - ber me this way. And I'll be

Bridge:

right be - hind__ your shoul - der watch - ing you. I'll be

From the Universal Motion Picture "SCHINDLER'S LIST"

THEME FROM "SCHINDLER'S LIST"

Composed by
JOHN WILLIAMS

Theme From "Schindler's List" - 2 - 1

Theme From "Schindler's List" - 2 - 2

A SOFT PLACE TO FALL

Words and Music by
ALLISON MOORER and GWIL OWEN

A Soft Place to Fall - 4 - 1

Verse 2:
Don't misunderstand me, baby, please.
I didn't mean to bring back memories.
You should have known the reason why I called.
I was looking for a soft place to fall.
(To Chorus:)

Verse 3:
Looking out your window at the dawn,
Baby, when you wake up, I'll be gone.
You're the one who taught me, after all,
How to find a soft place to fall.

A PERFECT MURDER
(Main Title)

Composed by
JAMES NEWTON HOWARD

Slowly ♩ = 80

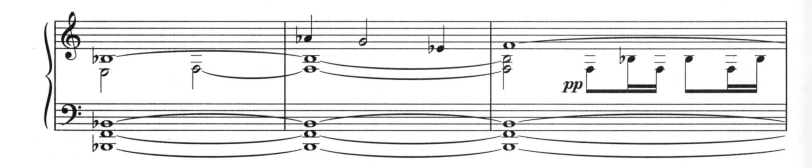

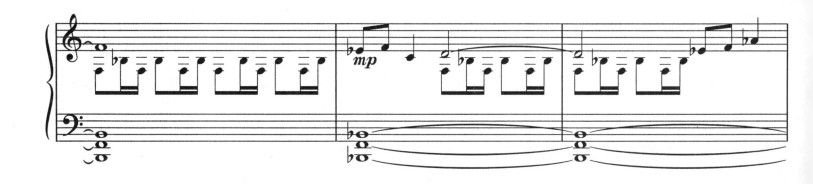

A Perfect Murder - 3 - 1

Slower

simile

SPACE JAM

Words and Music by
JAY McGOWAN, NATHANIEL ORANGE
and MICHAEL PHILLIPS

Moderately fast hip-hop ♩ = 126

Ev - 'ry - bod - y get up,___ it's time to slam now. We got the real jam

go - in' down. Wel - come to the Space Jam. Here's your

chance,___ do your dance___ at the Space Jam, al - right.

C - 'mon and slam and wel-come to the jam.

Space Jam - 9 - 1

Space Jam - 9 - 2

Space Jam - 9 - 3

Rap Section A:

wel - come to the jam. C - 'mon and slam if you wan- na jam.

⊕ *Coda* *Rap Section B:*

right. *See additional lyrics*

Space Jam. Here's your chance,__ do your dance__ at the

Space Jam, al - right.

Rap Section C:

See additional lyrics

1.

2. 3. 4. etc. *Repeat ad lib. and fade*

Verse 1 Rap:

Party people in the house, let's go.
It's your boy Jayski, a 'ight doe.
Pass that thing and watch me flex
Behind my back. You know what's next.
Just jam all in yo face,
What's up! Just fill the bass.
Droppin', knockin' down the room.
Shake it, quake it, space kaboom.
Just work that body, work that body.
Make sure you don't hurt nobody.
Get wild and lose your mind.
Take that thing into overtime.
Hey D. J., turn it up.
CD's gonna burn it up.
Come on y'all, get on the floor.
So hey, let's go, alright!
(To Chorus:)

Verse 2 Rap:

Slam, bam, thank you, ma'am.
Get on the floor and jam.
It's the Q-C-D on the microphone,
Girl, you got me in the zone.
Come on, come on, let's star the game.
Break it down, tell me your name.
You the team, I'm the coach.
Let's dance all night from coast to coast.
Just slide from left to right.
Just slide yourself tonight.
The Q-C-D droppin' bass.
Bringin' forth Quad in yo face.
Jam on it, let's have some fun.
Jam on it, one on one.
You run the O and I'll run the the D,
So come on, baby, just jam for me.
(To Chorus:)

Rap Section A:

Come on, it's time to get hype, say, "Hoop, there it is!"
Come on, all the fellas sayin', "Hoop, there it is!"
Come on, watch out for the ladies sayin', "Hoop, there it is!"
All the fellas sayin' whoop, there it is, hog!

Come on and run, baby, run.
Come on, come on, show 'em,
Run, baby, run.
Yeah, you wanna hoop, so shoot, baby, shoot.
Uh, it's time to hoop, so shoot, baby, shoot, baby.

Come on and slam and welcome to the jam.
Come on and slam if you wanna jam.
Come on and slam and welcome to the jam.
Come on and slam if you wanna jam.
(To Verse 2:)

Rap Section B:

Hey Ladies? (Yeah?) Y'all ready to start? (No!)
And y'all wanna know why? (Why?)
This is the slam jam.
Hey fellas? (Yo!) Y'all ready to start? (No!)
Y'all wanna know why? (Why?)
Yo, it's time to slam jam.
(To Chorus:)

Rap Section C:

C'mon, everybody say nah, nah, nah, nah, nah.
C'mon, c'mon, let me here you say hey, ey, ey, yo.
C'mon, c'mon, everybody, nah, nah, nah, nah, nah.
Just take the time to let me say hey, ey, ey, yo.
Check it out, a-check it out, y'all ready for this?
(You know it!) Na, y'all ain't ready.
Y'all ready for this? (You know it!)
C'mon, check it out.
Y'all ready to jam? (You know it!)
I, I, I don't think so.
Y'all ready to jam? (You know it!)
C'mon!

SOMEBODY BIGGER THAN YOU AND I

Words and Music by
JOHNNY LANGE, HY HEATH
and SONNY BURKE

Who made the moun-tain, who made the tree, Who made the riv-er flow to the sea, And who hung the moon in the star-ry sky? SOME-BOD-Y BIG-GER THAN YOU AND I.

Who makes the flow-ers bloom in the spring, Who writes the song for the rob-in to sing, And who sends the rain when the earth is dry? SOME-BOD-Y BIG-GER THAN

Somebody Bigger Than You and I - 2 - 1

A SONG FOR MAMA

Words and Music by
KENNETH "BABYFACE" EDMONDS

Verse:

1. You taught me ev-'ry-thing, and ev-'ry-thing you've giv-en me, I al-ways keep it in - side.
2. You're al - ways down for me, have al-ways been a - round for me, e - ven when I was _ bad.

A Song for Mama - 6 - 1

ooh, you know I love you, ma - ma. ____ Ma - ma, you're the queen of my heart. ____

____ Your love is like tears from the stars. ____

Ma - ma, I just want you to know, ____

To Coda

lov - ing you __ is like food to my soul. __

lov - ing you __ is like food to my soul. __

Bridge:

Nev - er gon - na go a day with - out you. __

From the Original Motion Picture Soundtrack "REALITY BITES"

STAY (I MISSED YOU)

Words and Music by
LISA LOEB

*Gtr. should capo 1st fret if matching the original recording key of D♭.

Stay (I Missed You) - 6 - 1

STREETS OF PHILADELPHIA

Words and Music by
BRUCE SPRINGSTEEN

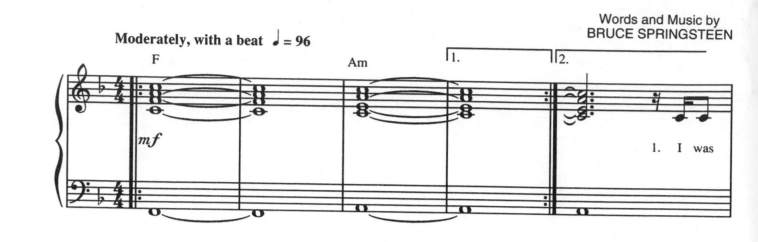

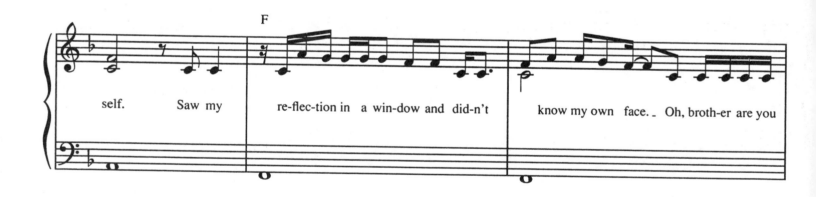

Streets of Philadelphia - 3 - 1

(L.H. cue notes 2nd & 3rd time)

la___ la la la la
la___ la la la la
la___ la la la la.___

To Coda ⊕

La___ la la la la
la___ la la la la
la___ la la la la

1.   2.   *Bridge:*

la___ la la 2. I walked the
cresc.
la___ la la la la.___
Ain't no an - gel gon-na greet
f

me;___
it's just you and I,___ my___ friend.___

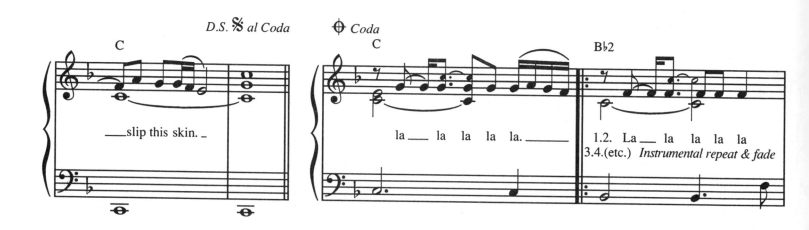

Verse 2:
I walked the avenue till my legs felt like stone.
I heard the voices of friends vanished and gone.
At night I could hear the blood in my veins
Just as black and whispering as the rain
On the streets of Philadelphia.
(To Chorus:)

Verse 3:
The night has fallen. I'm lyin' awake.
I can feel myself fading away.
So, receive me, brother, with your faithless kiss,
Or will we leave each other alone like this
On the streets of Philadelphia?
(To Chorus:)

From the Twentieth Century Fox Motion Picture

THERE'S SOMETHING ABOUT MARY

Words and Music by
JONATHAN RICHMAN

There's Something About Mary - 3 - 1

Verse 2:

TAKE ME TO THE RIVER

Words and Music by
AL GREEN and MABON HODGES

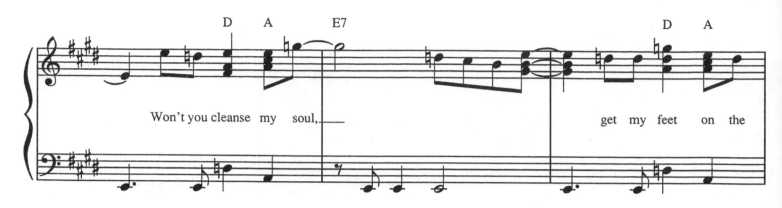

Won't you cleanse my soul,_____ get my feet on the

To Coda ⊕ 1. 2. To Next Strain 3. D.S.S. 𝄋𝄋 al Coda

ground.

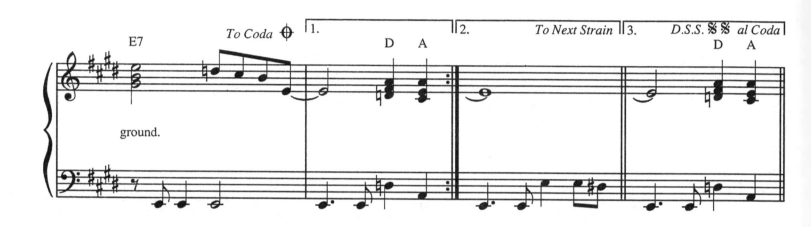

Bridge:

Hold__ me, love__ me, squeeze__ me,_____

tease__ me till I die,_____ till I die.__

THEMES FROM "BATMAN FOREVER"
(Main Title/Rooftop Seduction Theme)

Composed by
ELLIOT GOLDENTHAL
Arranged by RANDY KERBER

Themes from "Batman Forever" - 4 - 1

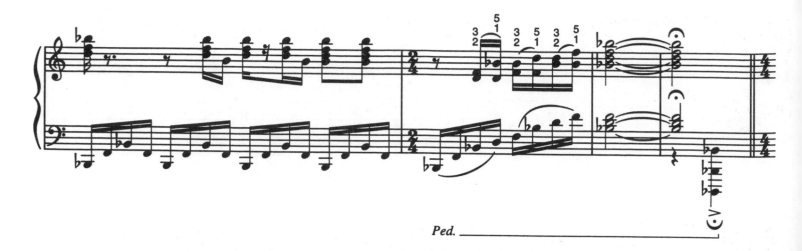

Rooftop Seduction Theme

Sultry & sensuous ♩ = 78

A tempo

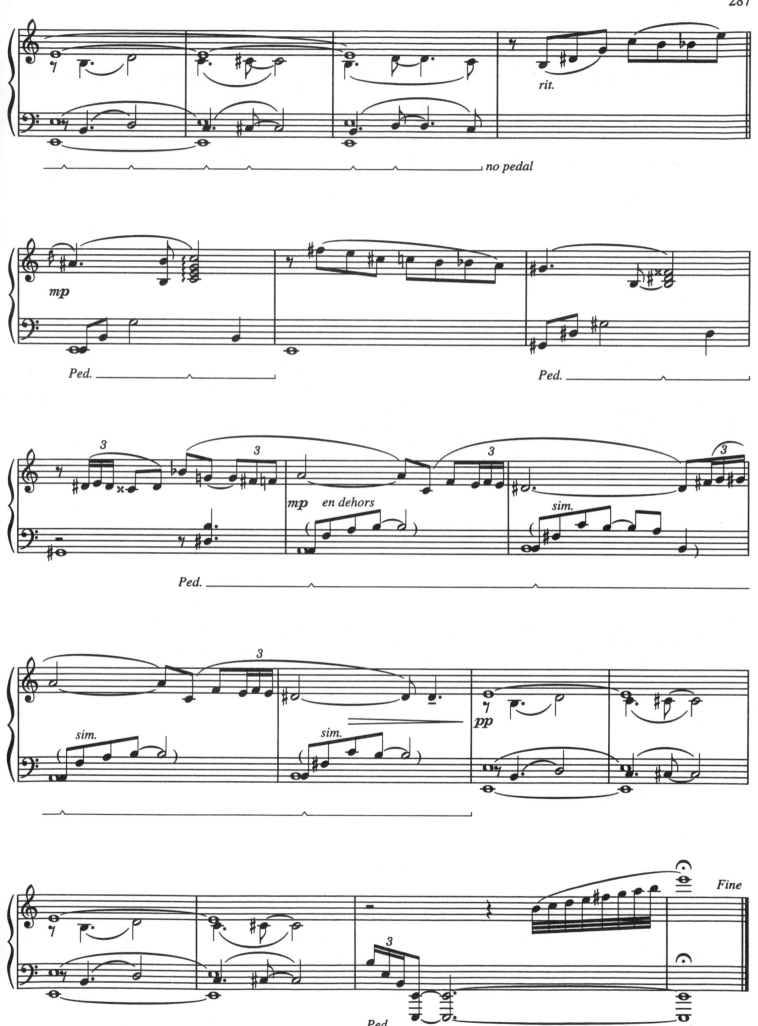

THEME FROM INSPECTOR GADGET

Words and Music by
HAIM SABAN and SHUKI LEVY

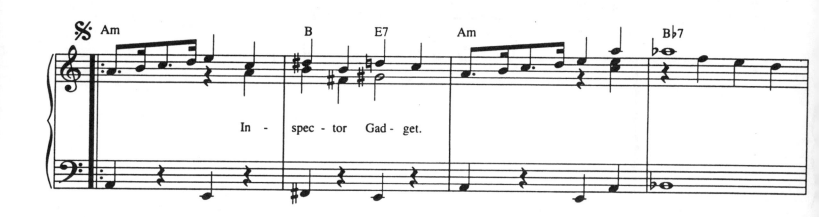

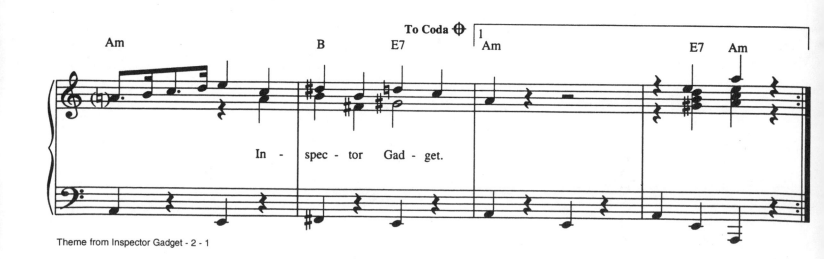

Theme from Inspector Gadget - 2 - 1

Theme from Inspector Gadget - 2 - 2

THEME FROM "JURASSIC PARK"

Composed by
JOHN WILLIAMS

Theme From "Jurassic Park" - 4 - 1

Theme From "Jurassic Park" - 4 - 2

Theme From "Jurassic Park" - 4 - 4

THEMES FROM "GRUMPIER OLD MEN"

("What the Heck" / "End Title")

Music by
ALAN SILVESTRI

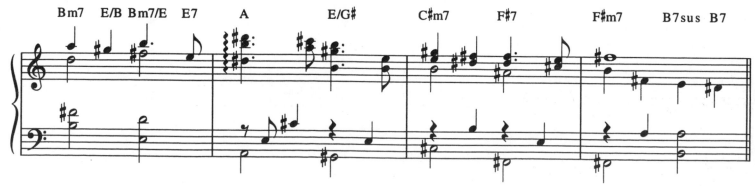

Themes from "Grumpier Old Men" - 6 - 2

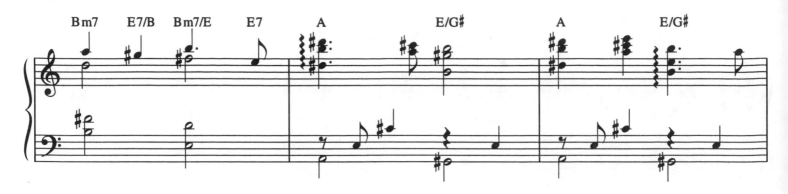

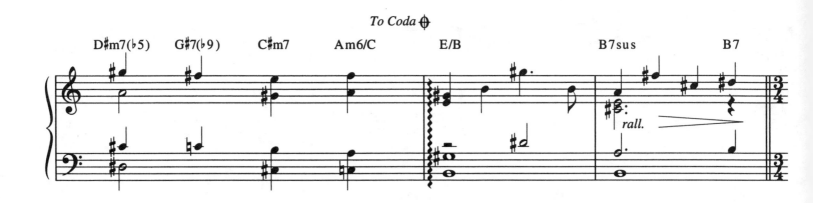

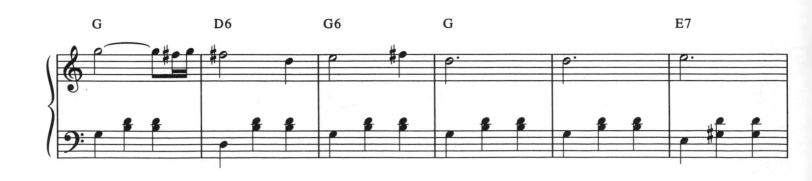

TIL I HEAR IT FROM YOU

Words and Music by JESSE VALENZUELA,
ROBIN WILSON and MARSHALL CRENSHAW

Moderate rock ♩ = 128

1. I did-n't ask,___ they should-n't have told___ me. At first I'd laugh,_ but now_
2. It gets hard___ when mem - o-ry's fad - ed is what_ they say._
(Harmony 2nd time only)

___ it's sink-in' in___ fast, what-ev - er they sold___ me. But ba - by,
___ It's like-ly they're___ just jeal-ous and jad - ed. But may-be } I don't wan-na

Til I Hear It from You - 5 - 1

Chorus:

take ad-vice_ from fools.__ I'll just fig-ure ev-'ry-thing_ is cool__ un-til I hear_

__ it from_____ you.

(Hear it from__ you.____)

2. Un-til I hear_ it from_____ you.

(Hear it from__ you.____)

Bridge:

I can't let it get__ me off,__ or break up__ my train_

TWISTER
(Main Theme)

By MARK MANCINA

Moderately fast ♩ = 120

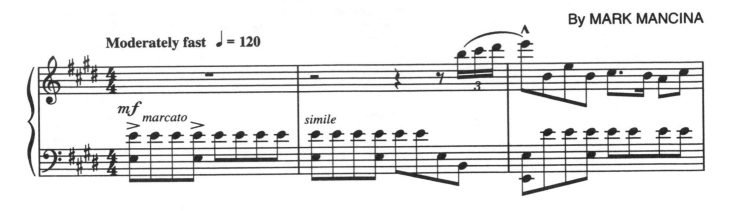

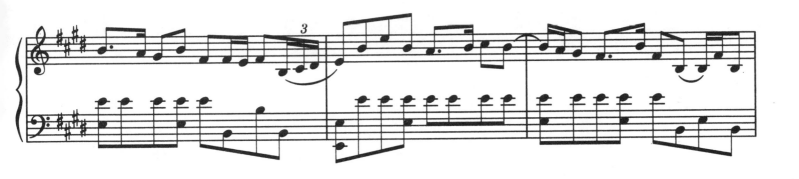

Twister - 3 - 1

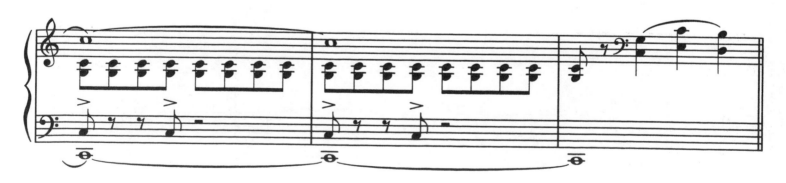

TUNE FOR DA
(From "THE BUTCHER BOY")

Composed by
ELLIOT GOLDENTHAL

Slowly (♩ = 66)

Tune for Da - 2 - 1

Tune for Da - 2 - 2

From "CITY of ANGELS"

THE UNFEELING KISS

By
GABRIEL YARED

Moderately fast (♩ = 80)
"Central Market"

(with pedal)

The Unfeeling Kiss - 6 - 1

Slowly (♩ = 80)

"An Angel Falls"

p

314

Slower (♩ = 70)

"The Unfeeling Kiss"

THE VICTOR

Composed by
JERRY GOLDSMITH

Slowly ♩ = 63

The Victor - 3 - 1

Piú mosso

simile

WHAT ABOUT US

Words and Music by
MISSY ELLIOTT and TIM MOSLEY

1. Ba-by, I've seen you   with an-oth-er
2. *See additional lyrics*

What About Us - 5 - 1

Verse 2:
Baby, I know that you've been pimpin'
Mr. Baller, trickin'.
Why'd you have to go, go and leave me?
Baby, I've always been your baby.
Love make a girl go crazy.
I can't understand why you left me.
(To Chorus:)

From the 20th Century-Fox Motion Picture "SHE'S THE ONE"

WALLS
(Circus)

Words and Music by
TOM PETTY

Moderately ♩ = 100

Verse:

1. Some days are dia - monds,
2. And all a - round your is - land,
3. *(Inst. solo ad lib....*

some days are rocks.___ Some doors are o-
there's a bar - ri - cade.___ It keeps out the dan-

- pen, some roads are blocked.___
- ger, yet holds in the pain.___
  ...end solo)

Walls - 4 - 1

WE'RE NOT MAKING LOVE ANYMORE

Words and Music by
DIANE WARREN and MICHAEL BOLTON

331

We're Not Making Love Anymore - 6 - 4

WHEN WE WERE KINGS

Words and Music by
ANDY MARVEL, ARNIE ROMAN
and AMY POWERS

When We Were Kings - 4 - 1

335

WHEREVER WOULD I BE

Words and Music by
DIANE WARREN

Moderate Rock Ballad

When my world is turn-ing, when it's turn-ing up-side down,___
When the dreams I dream,_ all seem a mil-lion miles a - way,___

when all I see is rain,
when I'm sure I'll nev-er win,

when I think the night won't end,_
when it's look-ing like I've lost my faith,_

Wherever Would I Be - 4 - 1

WHY SHOULD I CARE

Words by
CAROLE BAYER SAGER and
LINDA THOMPSON

Music by
CLINT EASTWOOD

Slowly ♩ = 72

(with pedal)

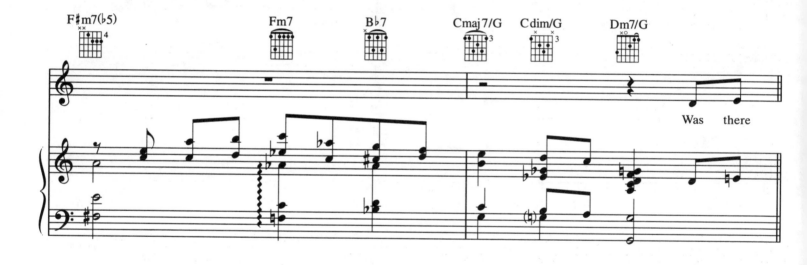

Was there

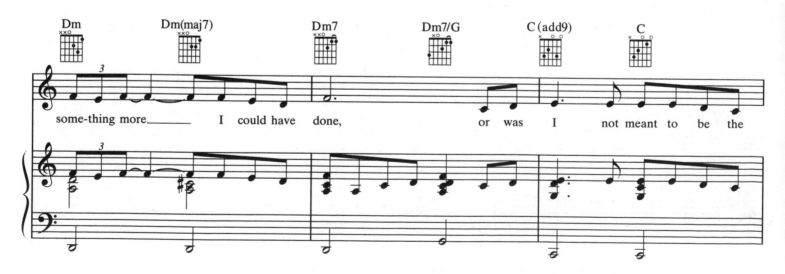

some-thing more___ I could have done, or was I not meant to be the

Why Should I Care - 4 - 1

YOU MUST LOVE ME

Words by
TIM RICE

Music by
ANDREW LLOYD WEBBER

Flowing ♩=92

1. Where do we go from here?
2. (See additional lyrics)

This is-n't where we in-tend-ed to be.___ We had it all,___ you be-lieved ___ in me,___ I be-lieved ___ in you.___

You Must Love Me - 3 - 1

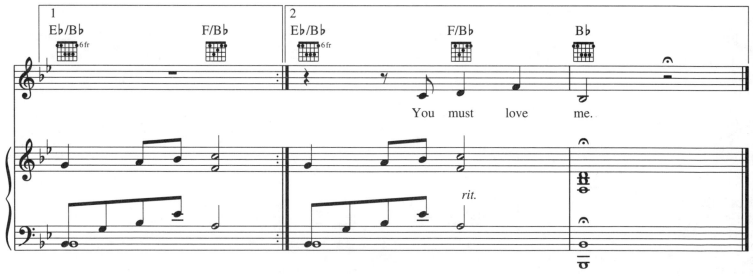

Additional Lyrics

Verse 2: *(Instrumental 8 bars)*
Why are you at my side?
How can I be any use to you now?
Give me a chance and I'll let you see how
Nothing has changed.
Deep in my heart I'm concealing
Things that I'm longing to say,
Scared to confess what I'm feeling
Frightened you'll slip away,
You must love me.

80 Years of Popular Music

This brilliant new series from Warner Bros. Publications collects the biggest singles and sheet music sellers for each decade. Each book contains:

- **Exciting colorful covers** • **Dozens of #1 and Top 10 hit songs**
- **The best artists and best music ever** • **A special historical overview of each decade** • **Great price**

The whole series makes great collectibles and contains music your customers already know and love. They'll use these books year after year. Stock up today!

The Thirties

Piano/Vocal/Chords
(MF9824)
ISBN 0-7692-6722-X UPC 0-29156-95403-6

Titles in this 47-song collection include: **Anything Goes • As Time Goes By • Begin the Beguine • Blue Moon • Brother Can You Spare a Dime • For All We Know • Hooray for Hollywood • I Got Rhythm • I Only Have Eyes for You • It Don't Mean a Thing (If It Ain't Got That Swing) • It's Only a Paper Moon • I'm in the Mood for Love • Mood Indigo • Over the Rainbow • Sophisticated Lady • Stars Fell on Alabama • You and the Night and the Music** and more.

The Forties

Piano/Vocal/Chords
(MF9825)
ISBN 0-7692-6723-8 UPC 0-29156-95404-3

Titles in this 57-song collection include: **Autumn Serenade • Blues in the Night • Chattanooga Choo Choo • Don't Fence Me In • Don't Get Around Much Anymore • Don't Sit Under the Apple Tree (With Anyone Else But Me) • Fools Rush In • I Got It Bad and That Ain't Good • I'll Walk Alone • Laura • New York, New York • Pennsylvania 6-5000 • Rum and Coca-Cola • Shangri-La • Two O'Clock Jump • You Stepped Out of a Dream** and more.

The Fifties

Piano/Vocal/Chords
(MF9826)
ISBN 0-7692-6724-6 UPC 0-29156-95405-0

Titles in this 72-song collection include: **All I Have to Do Is Dream • Be-Bop-A-Lula • Bye Bye, Love • Catch a Falling Star • Chantilly Lace • Earth Angel • Good Golly Miss Molly • I Only Have Eyes for You • I'm Walkin' • La Bamba • Let the Good Times Roll • The Lion Sleeps Tonight (Wimoweh) • Lonely Boy • My Boy Lollipop • (We're Gonna) Rock Around the Clock • Shout • Splish Splash • Teen Angel • Wake Up Little Susie • Why Do Fools Fall in Love • Your Cheatin' Heart** and more.

The Twenties

Piano/Vocal/Chords
(MF9823)
ISBN 0-7692-6721-1 UPC 0-29156-95402-9

Titles in this 52-song collection include: **Ain't Misbehavin' • Ain't She Sweet • Bye Bye Blackbird • Charleston • Five Foot Two, Eyes of Blue • Happy Days Are Here Again • Ida, Sweet as Apple Cider • If You Knew Susie (Like I Knew Susie) • I'm Just Wild About Harry • I'm Sitting on Top of the World • Love Me or Leave Me • Makin' Whoopee! • My Blue Heaven • Someone to Watch Over Me • Sweet Georgia Brown • Tea for Two • When You're Smiling** and more.

AD0153